JOHN THE BAPTIST

MATTHEW 3; 14:1-12; MARK 1:1-9; 6:17-29; LUKE 3:1-21; 7:19-23; JOHN 1:19-35
FOR CHILDREN

Written by Ronald Klug
Illustrated by Betty Wind

Former Title:
THE STRANGE YOUNG MAN IN THE DESERT

ARCH Books
COPYRIGHT © 1971, 1984 CONCORDIA PUBLISHING HOUSE
3558 S. Jefferson Avenue, St. Louis, MO 63118
MANUFACTURED IN THE UNITED STATES OF AMERICA
ISBN 0-570-06189-X

In old King Herod's wicked days,
as Isaiah had foretold,
there appeared in the desert a strange
young man
with a voice that was strong and bold.

He wore rough clothes of camel's hair
with a leather belt tied round.
He ate wild honey and locusts for food
and slept in a cave underground.

He was not afraid in the desert wild,
because he trusted in God.
When people heard of the way he lived,
they thought him a little bit odd.

One day this John began to speak;
in the desert his voice rang clear.
From villages, cities, and neighboring towns
the people came out to hear.

John preached,
"It's time you changed your ways.
Repent, start doing what's right.
Come down to the river
and be baptized.
God's kingdom is coming
with might."
The people came,
and some of them
asked, "Tell us,
are *you* the King?"
But John cried,
'No! I'm not the One.
It's news
of Him I bring."

Then one day
Jesus, the King
walked by
and John said
"Look at Him
Behold
the Lamb of God is here!
He'll take away your sin."

While John was teaching
on Jordan's bank,
Jesus came by to see.
"Baptize Me," said Jesus.
But John said, "What?
You should baptize me!"

Jesus replied, "Do as I say."
And finally John agreed.
He baptized Jesus there in the river,
and a strange thing happened indeed.

The Spirit of God came down from heaven,
came in the shape of a dove.
And the voice of God, like thunder, said,
"This is My Son, whom I love."

Then Jesus and John came out of
the water, and Jesus went on
His way. John kept teaching and
told the people all that had
happened that day.

Now old King Herod did a wicked thing:
he married his brother's wife.
Brave John told Herod that he was wrong
to live such a sinful life.

The king didn't like to be told
so he called his soldiers in.
"Go find this John, and throw
Enough of this talk about sin!

was wrong,

in jail!

John was captured, sat long in jail
till he wondered about one thing.
He sent some friends to Jesus to ask,
"Are you really Christ, the King?"

"Tell John to look at the things I do,"
said Jesus to the men.
"The deaf can hear; the lame can walk,
and blind men see again."

John's friends returned
to tell him the news
and listen to John's reply.
"I trust this Jesus.
He's God's own Son.
Now I'm not afraid to die."

King Herod invited his friends and lords
to a feast in his royal hall.
Salome danced as they ate and drank.
Her dancing pleased them all.

Her dance so pleased
old Herod the king
that he said,
"Now listen to this:
Salome can have
whatever she wants,
and if half the
kingdom it is."

But Herod was sad
when he heard her reply,
for she talked to
her mother and said:
"I want nothing less
than to have John killed
and for you to give me his head."

So John was killed,
and his good friends came
and buried him in a tomb.
They met and prayed
and talked and cried.
Their faces were
filled with gloom.

"What shall we do now?" they asked themselves.
"John, our leader, is dead."
They looked bewildered till one spoke out,
"Remember what John said?
'Behold the Lamb of God,' he said
as Jesus was walking by.
Let's go to Jesus, follow Him,
and serve Him till we die."

DEAR PARENTS:

This book uses the New Testament accounts to tell the story of *John the Baptist.*

His birth was strange. The angel Gabriel appeared to the aged priest Zechariah to announce, "Your wife Elizabeth will bear you a son, and you shall call his name John." John was to prepare the way for the Lord, as the Old Testament prophets had said.

His ways were strange: camel's hair clothes, locusts and wild honey for food, desert for his home.

His message was strange. He spoke for God, calling people to repent and to believe in God because His kingdom was coming.

He was strange because he accepted no honors for himself. He pointed to Jesus and called Him "the Lamb of God who takes away the sins of the world."

He was strange because he was willing to risk his own life to do what he thought was right before God. He reminded King Herod that it was a sin to take his brother's wife. He suffered prison and execution by the sword because He remained faithful to God.

He seemed strange then, but now we know John was not so strange. He knew what God had called him to do. He talked, lived, and died to bring people to Jesus, their Savior.

THE EDITOR